Let's Do It

by Cole Porter

Let's Do It

by Cole Porter

with illustrations by Ward Schumaker

CHRONICLE BOOKS

SAN FRANCISCO

Text copyright © 1928 Warner Bros. Inc. (ASCAP) (renewed). All rights reserved.
Illustrations © 1993 by Ward Schumaker. All rights reserved.
No part of this book may be reproduced in any form without written
permission from the publisher.

Publisher gratefully acknowledges the cooperation of
The Cole Porter Musical and Literary Property Trusts
and Warner/Chappell Music, Inc.

Printed in Hong Kong.
ISBN 0-8118-0448-8
Library of Congress Cataloging-in-Publication Data available.

Cover image: Ward Schumaker
Book design: Gretchen Scoble

Distributed in Canada by Raincoast Books,
112 East Third Avenue, Vancouver, B.C. V5T 1C8

10 9 8 7 6 5 4 3 2 1

Chronicle Books
275 Fifth Street
San Francisco, CA 94103

When the little bluebird,
Who has never said a word,
Starts to sing "Spring, spring,"
When the little bluebell,
In the bottom of the dell,
Starts to ring "Ding, ding,"

When the little blue clerk,
In the middle of his work,
Starts a tune to the moon up above,
It is nature, that's all,
Simply telling us to fall
In love.

Birds do it, bees do it,
Even educated fleas do it,
Let's do it, let's fall in love.
In Spain, the best upper sets do it,
Lithuanians and Letts do it,

Let's do it, let's fall in love.

The Dutch in old Amsterdam do it,
Not to mention the Finns,
Folks in Siam do it,
Think of Siamese twins.
Some Argentines, without means, do it,
People say, in Boston, even beans do it,

Let's do it, let's fall in love.

Ye Olde Boston Beans

The nightingales, in the dark, do it,
Larks, k-razy for a lark, do it,
Let's do it, let's fall in love.
Canaries, caged in the house, do it,
When they're out of season,
　　grouse do it,

Let's do it, let's fall in love.

The most sedate barnyard fowls do it,
When a chanticleer cries,
High-browed old owls do it,
They're supposed to be wise,
Penguins in flocks,
     on the rocks, do it,
Even little cuckoos,
     in their clocks, do it,

Let's do it, let's fall in love.

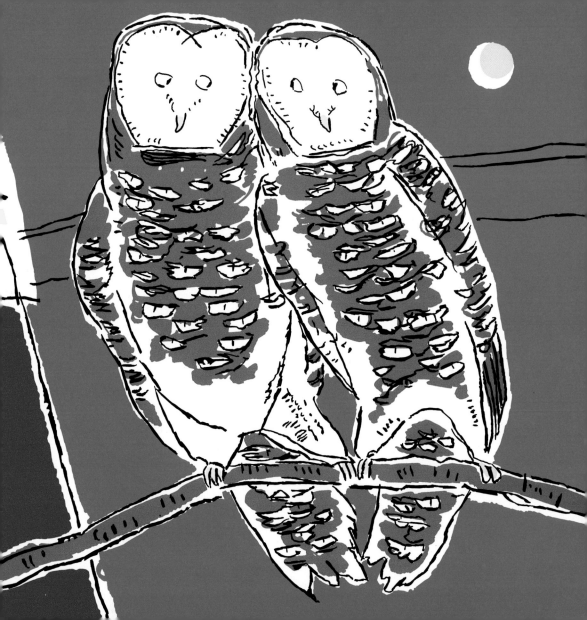

Romantic sponges, they say, do it,
Oysters, down in Oyster Bay, do it,
Let's do it, let's fall in love.
Cold Cape Cod clams, 'gainst their wish, do it,
Even lazy jellyfish do it,

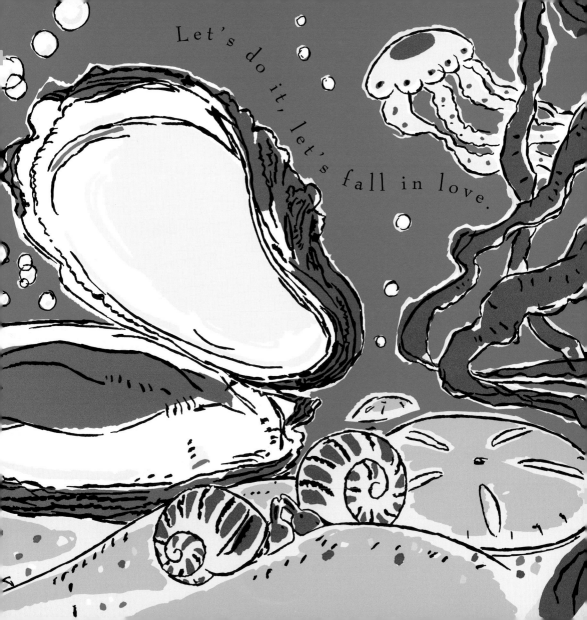

Let's do it, let's fall in love.

Electric eels, I might add, do it,
Though it shocks 'em, I know.
Why ask if shad do it?
Waiter, bring me shad roe.

In shallow shoals, English soles do it,
Goldfish, in the privacy of bowls, do it,

Let's do it, let's fall in love.

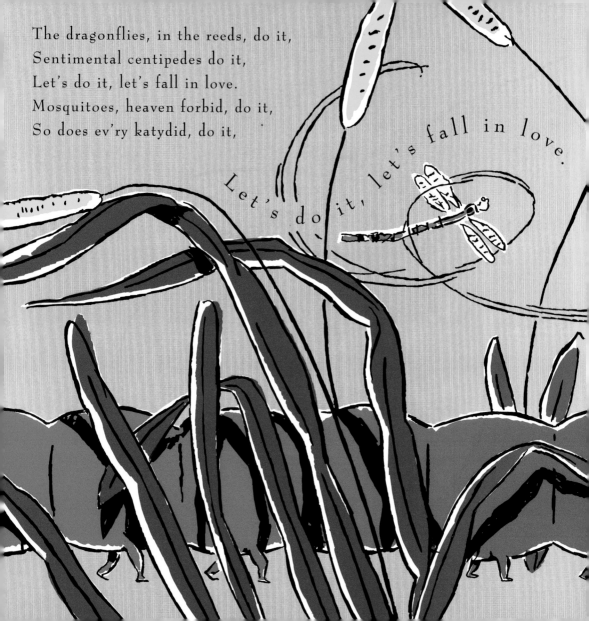

The dragonflies, in the reeds, do it,
Sentimental centipedes do it,
Let's do it, let's fall in love.
Mosquitoes, heaven forbid, do it,
So does ev'ry katydid, do it,

Let's do it, let's fall in love.

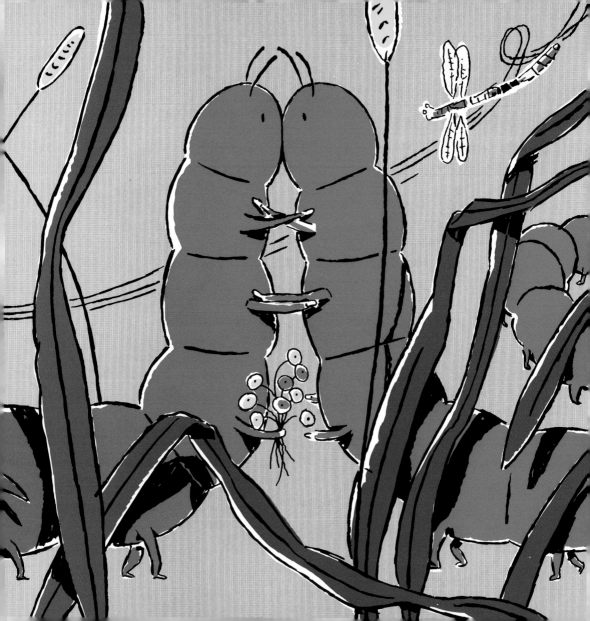

The most refined lady bugs do it,
When a gentleman calls,
Moths in your rugs, do it,
What's the use of moth balls?
Locusts in trees do it, bees do it,
Even overeducated fleas do it,

Let's do it, let's fall in love.

The chimpanzees, in the zoos, do it,
Some courageous kangaroos do it,
Let's do it, let's fall in love.

I'm sure giraffes, on the sly, do it,
Heavy hippopotami do it,

Let's do it, let's fall in love.

Old sloths who hang down from twigs do it,
Though the effort is great,
Sweet guinea pigs do it,
Buy a couple and wait.
The world admits bears in pits do it,
Even pekineses in the Ritz do it.

Let's do it, let's fall in love.